D1287492

DATE DUE

Small-Game Hunting
Rabbits, Squirrels, and Other Small Animals

Sloan MacRae

PowerKiDS press

New York

Open Season

Published in 2011 by The Rosen Publishing Group, Inc.
29 East 21st Street, New York, NY 10010

First Edition

Editor: Amelie von Zumbusch
Book Design: Greg Tucker
Photo Researcher: Jessica Gerweck

Photo Credits: Cover, pp. 5, 6, 7, 8, 9, 12–13, 14, 15, 18, 19, 22, 23, 28 Shutterstock.com; pp. 4, 10–11 © www.iStockphoto.com/Mark Jensen; pp. 16–17 © www.iStockphoto.com/Robert Gubbins; p. 20 © www.iStockphoto.com/Dietmar Klement; p. 21 © www.iStockphoto.com/Adventure Photo; p. 24 © www.iStockphoto.com/Nick Tzolov; p. 25 © www.iStockphoto.com/Brian Nolan; pp. 26–27 Image Source/Getty Images; p. 29 Jupiterimages/Getty Images.

Library of Congress Cataloging-in-Publication Data

MacRae, Sloan.
  Small-game hunting : rabbits, squirrels, and other small animals / Sloan MacRae. – 1st ed.
     p. cm. — (Open season)
  Includes index.
  ISBN 978-1-4488-0707-9 (library binding) — ISBN 978-1-4488-1375-9 (pbk.) —
ISBN 978-1-4488-1376-6 (6-pack)
  1. Small game hunting—United States—Juvenile literature. 2. Varmint hunting—United
States—Juvenile literature. I. Title.
  SK41.M33 2011
  799.2'5—dc22
                                    2010007054

Manufactured in the United States of America

CPSIA Compliance Information: Batch #WS10PK: For Further Information contact Rosen Publishing, New York, New York at 1-800-237-9932

Contents

Bigger Is Not Always Better

What kinds of animals do you picture when you think about hunting? Most people probably think of large animals, such as deer. Hunters enjoy the challenge of hunting big animals, but small game present challenges of their own.

You might think that small animals are easier

Some small-game hunters, such as this young man, use dogs to help them track down their hard-to-find prey.

This groundhog is hiding in its burrow, or underground home. Groundhogs are also known as woodchucks and marmots.

prey just because of their size. This is not always the case. They can use their small size to their advantage. Small animals are small **targets**. It is also easier for them to find places to hide. Have you ever tried to find a frightened animal that did not want to be seen? It is hard unless you know where and how to look.

Small game is a broad **category**. Some people consider any animal smaller than a deer to be small game. You should check the Web site of your state's game **agency** to find out which small game can be hunted. Your state might **classify**

Raccoons, such as the one seen here, are considered small game in many states.

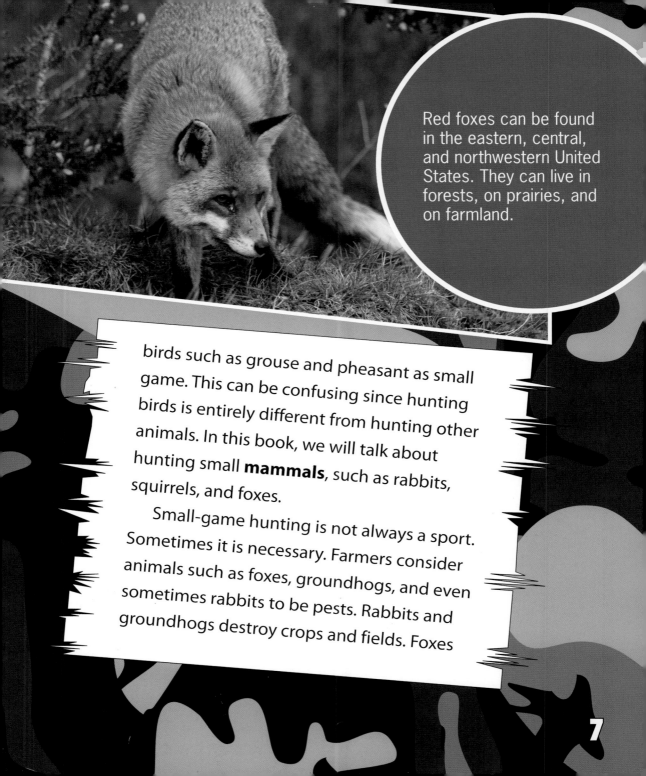

Red foxes can be found in the eastern, central, and northwestern United States. They can live in forests, on prairies, and on farmland.

birds such as grouse and pheasant as small game. This can be confusing since hunting birds is entirely different from hunting other animals. In this book, we will talk about hunting small **mammals**, such as rabbits, squirrels, and foxes.

Small-game hunting is not always a sport. Sometimes it is necessary. Farmers consider animals such as foxes, groundhogs, and even sometimes rabbits to be pests. Rabbits and groundhogs destroy crops and fields. Foxes

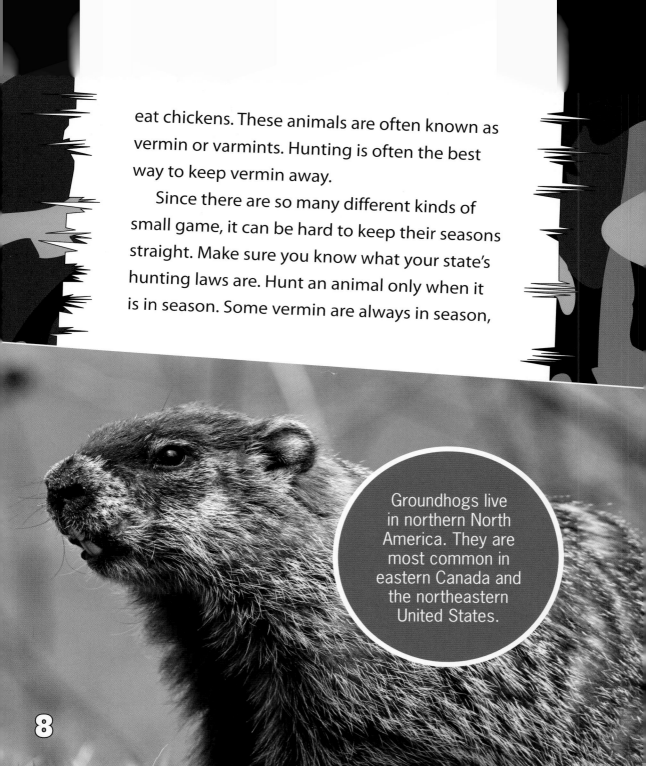

eat chickens. These animals are often known as vermin or varmints. Hunting is often the best way to keep vermin away.

Since there are so many different kinds of small game, it can be hard to keep their seasons straight. Make sure you know what your state's hunting laws are. Hunt an animal only when it is in season. Some vermin are always in season,

Groundhogs live in northern North America. They are most common in eastern Canada and the northeastern United States.

This is a gray squirrel. There are several kinds of gray squirrels in the United States, including eastern gray squirrels and western gray squirrels.

but make sure that you know your state's laws before you go hunting. Imagine you are hunting squirrels, and you have a perfect shot at a rabbit. What if the rabbit is not in season? Be certain before you shoot. Hunting animals that are not in season is against the law.

Mountain cottontails, such as this rabbit, are found mainly in the western United States. They are one of several kinds of North American cottontails.

The first thing you need to hunt is proof that you have passed a hunting safety course. These courses teach you the most important part of hunting, firearm safety. If you pass the test at the end of the course, you should be able to purchase a hunting **license** from your state.

Along with your license, it is a good idea to buy a warm jacket. Many hunting jackets have pockets that are deep enough to carry rabbits and squirrels.

This young hunter is well dressed for a day of small-game hunting. His jacket will keep him warm, while his orange vest will keep him safe.

One advantage of small-game hunting is that you can shoot more animals than you can in other kinds of hunting. Depending on the type of game, most states allow you to shoot several animals in a single day. The top number of animals you can kill is the bag limit. It is against the law to go over this limit.

Hunting Facts

Hunters wear blaze orange for safety. Wearing this color makes it easy for other hunters to see you.

Different game require different weapons. Most small-game hunters agree that shotguns are the best tools for hunting rabbits and squirrels. These animals are not only small, they are also fast. They scurry around. It would be unsafe to shoot at them with a rifle. Rifles shoot single bullets that cause lots of damage. They are also very **precise**. Shotguns are different. They scatter dozens of pellets, or shot, over a short range. This means that you must get closer to your prey, but you have a much better chance of hitting it.

This small-game hunter is using a shotgun. Hunters use shotguns to hunt other prey, such as game birds and waterfowl, as well as small game.

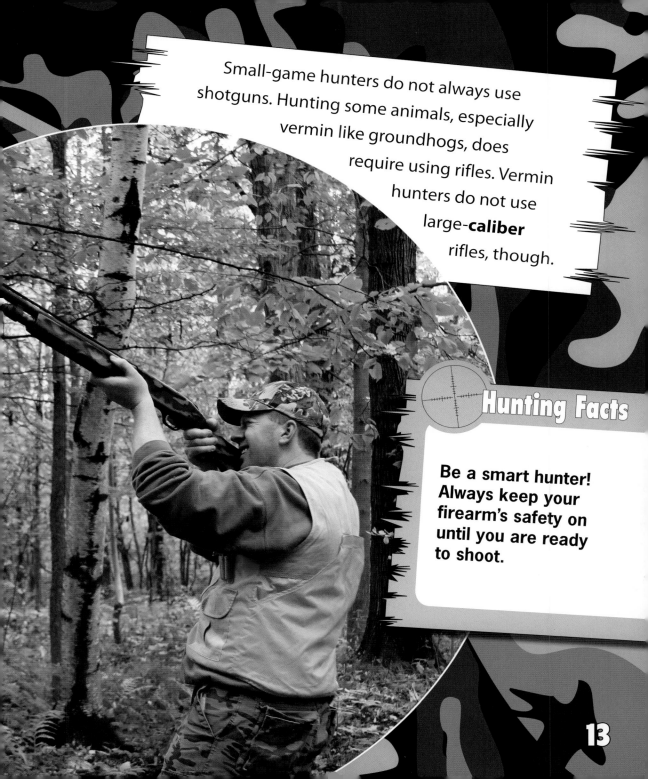

Small-game hunters do not always use shotguns. Hunting some animals, especially vermin like groundhogs, does require using rifles. Vermin hunters do not use large-**caliber** rifles, though.

Hunting Facts

Be a smart hunter! Always keep your firearm's safety on until you are ready to shoot.

This hunter is practicing firing his small-caliber rifle. Practicing at a shooting range is one of the best ways to become a better hunter.

The most common varmint rifle is probably the .22 caliber. It takes small **ammunition** and barely makes a noise when fired. Remember that even a .22 rifle must be handled with care.

Hunters looking for a greater challenge may prefer archery. It is very hard to hit a small

The kind of bow that this hunter is using is called a compound bow. Compound bows are the kind of bows most often used in hunting.

animal with an arrow. Arrows are slower than shot or bullets. The animal has much more time to move after the arrow is let go. Successful small-game archers have expert aim and lots of luck.

On the Hunt

Most hunters are guests on somebody else's property. You must always ask the owner for permission to hunt. Think about it. Would you want a bunch of strangers with guns wandering around your property?

There are also special areas called state game lands that are owned by the government. You are welcome to hunt on these lands, but be careful. Hikers and dog walkers also use state game lands, and they do not always wear blaze orange. Be sure of your target before you pull the **trigger**.

Always make sure you know who owns the land you are hunting on and double-check that you are allowed to hunt there.

Small game can be hard to find. Have you ever heard the folktale of Brer Rabbit? Like many folktales, it has made-up things, such as talking animals. However, it also has elements of truth. In the story, Brer

Hunting Facts

You have to be old enough to hunt. Most states have laws that require you to be at least 12.

Rabbit hides in a briar patch. The thick branches and thorns protect him and it is hard to get him to come out. Rabbits love to hide in heavy brush. Squirrels love to hide in trees. The trick is to get them to show themselves.

Raccoons most often hide in tree branches. However, they also hide in hollow trees, woodpiles, and holes in the ground.

Hunting small game is challenging because you need to be fairly close to your prey. You do not want to startle the animal when it is too far away. One method for hunting rabbits is to startle them out of their hiding places and into the open. You can do this by kicking and stomping in thick brush. Rabbits are easy to track if there is

This hare was frightened out of the bushes by a hunter. Hares are closely related to rabbits and are hunted using the same methods.

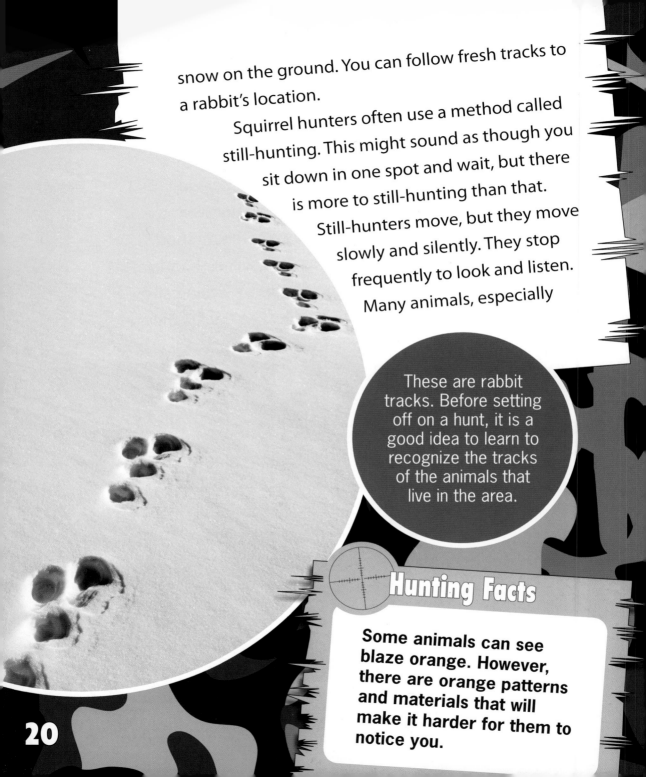

snow on the ground. You can follow fresh tracks to a rabbit's location.

Squirrel hunters often use a method called still-hunting. This might sound as though you sit down in one spot and wait, but there is more to still-hunting than that. Still-hunters move, but they move slowly and silently. They stop frequently to look and listen. Many animals, especially

These are rabbit tracks. Before setting off on a hunt, it is a good idea to learn to recognize the tracks of the animals that live in the area.

Hunting Facts

Some animals can see blaze orange. However, there are orange patterns and materials that will make it harder for them to notice you.

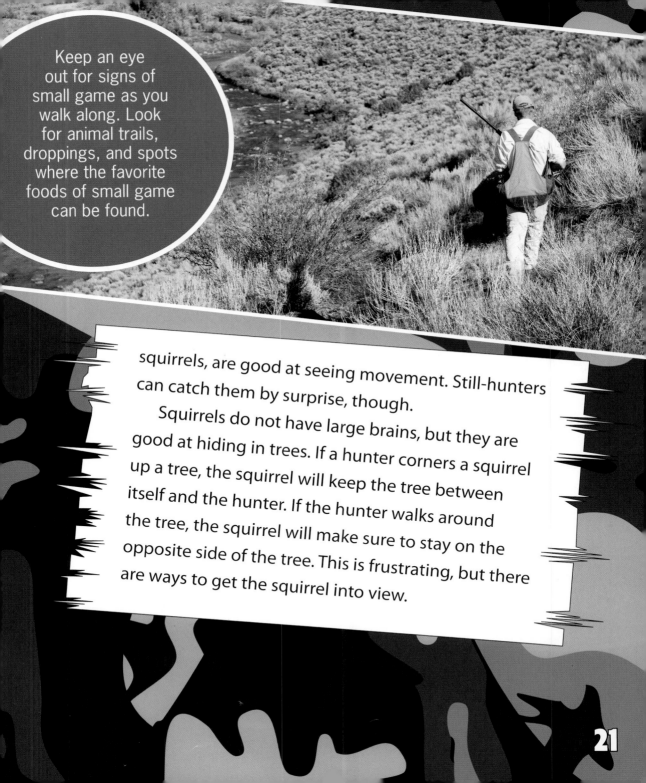

Keep an eye out for signs of small game as you walk along. Look for animal trails, droppings, and spots where the favorite foods of small game can be found.

squirrels, are good at seeing movement. Still-hunters can catch them by surprise, though.

Squirrels do not have large brains, but they are good at hiding in trees. If a hunter corners a squirrel up a tree, the squirrel will keep the tree between itself and the hunter. If the hunter walks around the tree, the squirrel will make sure to stay on the opposite side of the tree. This is frustrating, but there are ways to get the squirrel into view.

If you are hunting with two or more people, one hunter can stand absolutely still. Another hunter should walk around the tree. The squirrel will circle until the first hunter has a shot. If you are hunting on your own, you can try throwing a branch or some stones at the tree.

A squirrel's small, sharp claws are great at holding on to tree trunks and branches. Squirrels also have great balance, thanks, in part, to their tails.

Barking Up the Right Tree

Since small game can be hard to find, some hunters look for help. Dogs can be a big help to small-game hunters. A good hunting dog has a powerful sense of smell, excellent hunting **instincts**, and does not shy away from the sound of gunshots.

Dachshunds were first bred to hunt badgers. Today, they are used to hunt several kinds of small game, including rabbits and groundhogs.

Certain dogs are bred and trained to be excellent hunters. Beagles and hounds are especially good rabbit hunters. Hunting with beagles is so popular that it is often called beagling.

Raccoon hunting is very hard without the aid of dogs. Since raccoons are **nocturnal**, they are most often hunted at night. It is hard enough to find

Raccoons, such as this treed raccoon, are popular small-game targets. They are often hunted for their thick, soft fur.

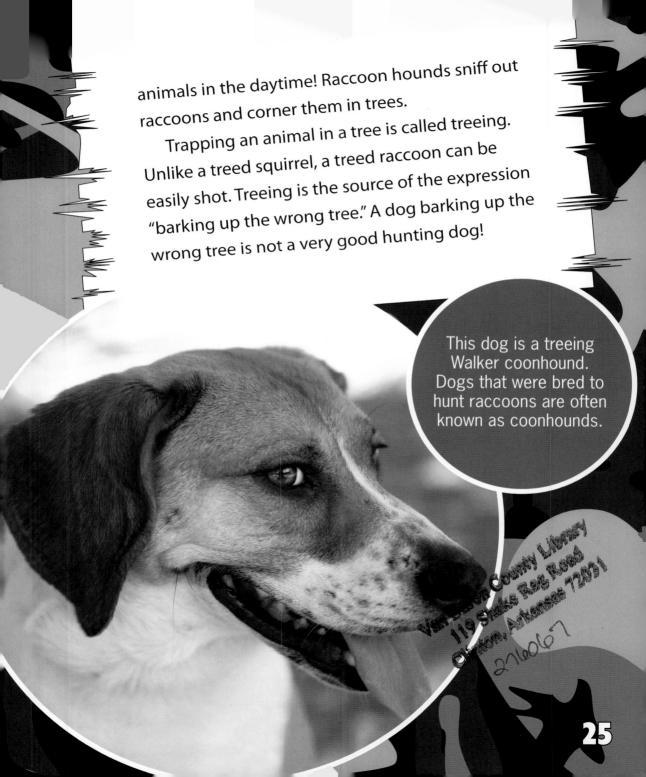

animals in the daytime! Raccoon hounds sniff out raccoons and corner them in trees.

Trapping an animal in a tree is called treeing. Unlike a treed squirrel, a treed raccoon can be easily shot. Treeing is the source of the expression "barking up the wrong tree." A dog barking up the wrong tree is not a very good hunting dog!

This dog is a treeing Walker coonhound. Dogs that were bred to hunt raccoons are often known as coonhounds.

Why We Hunt

Let's face it, rabbits are cute. Many people hate the idea of small animals being hunted for fun. These **activists** work hard to outlaw small-game hunting. However, it is worth remembering that nature is wild. Animals kill other animals. Human beings are animals, too. Most of us do not depend on hunting as we once did, but people in other parts of the world still hunt in order to eat. Not everyone has a neighborhood grocery store.

Hunting is a part of nature. Some kinds of small game, such as foxes, even hunt other sorts of small game, such as rabbits!

Most of the animals we consider vermin are only pests because there are too many of them. Predators such as wolves, grizzly bears, and bobcats are rare these days. They can no longer control the populations of

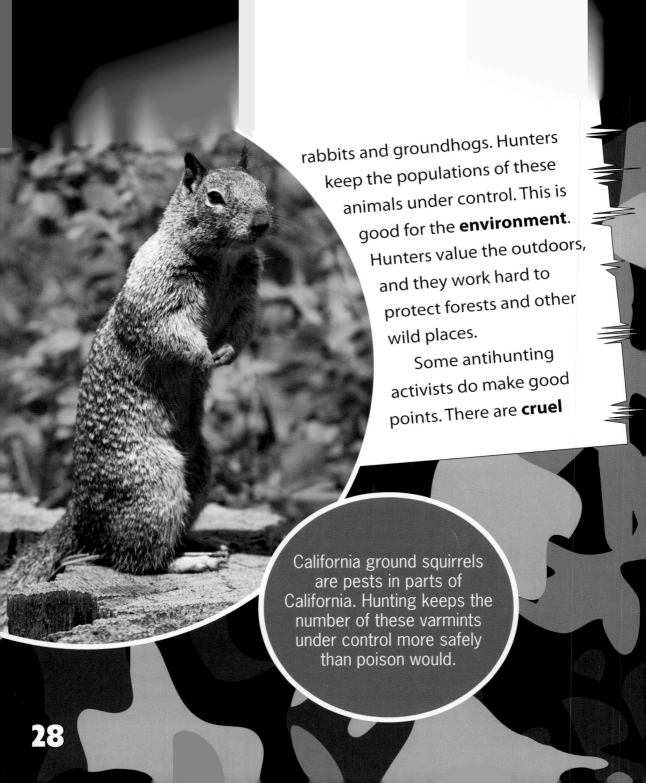

rabbits and groundhogs. Hunters keep the populations of these animals under control. This is good for the **environment**. Hunters value the outdoors, and they work hard to protect forests and other wild places.

Some antihunting activists do make good points. There are **cruel**

California ground squirrels are pests in parts of California. Hunting keeps the number of these varmints under control more safely than poison would.

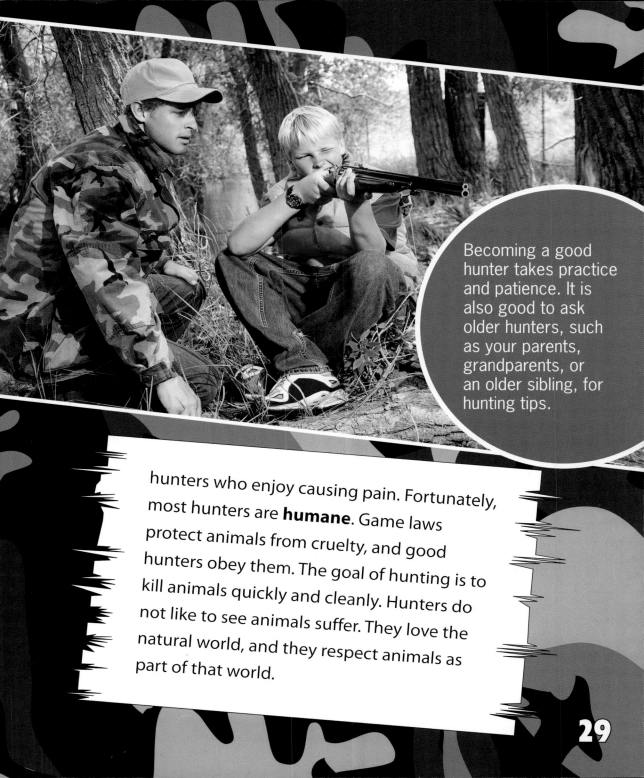

Becoming a good hunter takes practice and patience. It is also good to ask older hunters, such as your parents, grandparents, or an older sibling, for hunting tips.

hunters who enjoy causing pain. Fortunately, most hunters are **humane**. Game laws protect animals from cruelty, and good hunters obey them. The goal of hunting is to kill animals quickly and cleanly. Hunters do not like to see animals suffer. They love the natural world, and they respect animals as part of that world.

Happy Hunting

⊕ Getting lost is no fun. Make sure you know the area where you are hunting. Learn how to read a map and use a compass.

⊕ If you are hunting with a dog, always make sure you know where it is. It does not hurt to put some blaze orange on its collar.

⊕ Practice shooting before you go hunting. Do this in a safe place, such as a sporting club's shooting range.

⊕ Keep your eyes and ears open.

⊕ If you are not having luck finding small game, try a different area.

⊕ When hunting in a group, pay special attention to where your friends are. Your hunting safety course will teach you how to safely shoot with a group of hunters.

⊕ Carry your extra shells in a pocket that is easy to reach.

⊕ Never shoot until you are absolutely sure of the target.

⊕ You should field dress, or clean, an animal soon after you kill it. You do not want the meat to spoil.

⊕ Be safe!

Glossary

activists (AK-tih-vists) People who take action for what they believe is right.

agency (AY-jen-see) A special department of the government.

ammunition (am-yuh-NIH-shun) Things fired from weapons, such as bullets.

caliber (KA-luh-ber) Having to do with how wide a gun's opening is.

category (KA-teh-gor-ee) A group of things that are alike.

classify (KLA-seh-fy) To arrange in groups.

cruel (KROOL) Causing pain or suffering.

environment (en-VY-ern-ment) All the living things and conditions of a place.

humane (hyoo-MAYN) Kind or not causing pain.

instincts (IN-stinkts) The feelings every animal has that help it know what to do.

license (LY-suns) Official permission to do something.

mammals (MA-mulz) Warm-blooded animals that have backbones and hair, breathe air, and feed milk to their young.

nocturnal (nok-TUR-nul) Active during the night.

precise (prih-SYS) Exact.

targets (TAHR-gits) Things that are aimed at.

trigger (TRIH-ger) Something that is pulled or pressed to shoot a gun.

Index

Web Sites

Due to the changing nature of Internet links, PowerKids Press has developed an online list of Web sites related to the subject of this book. This site is updated regularly. Please use this link to access the list: www.powerkidslinks.com/os/sgh/